我们的感觉

Social Emotional and Multicultural Learning | Non-Fiction Series

Copyright © 2022 by Level Learning, INC. and Washington Yu Ying PCS™
Original and Edited Text Copyright © 2022 by Washington Yu Ying PCS™

All rights reserved. No part of this book in whole or part may be reproduced without written permission from the publisher.

Published by Level Learning, INC.

Content Contributors:
Washington Yu Ying PCS™
Level Learning - Cindy Chiang

Illustrations by: Thomas Watkins

Leveling classification based on Level Learning standard. For full description, visit www.levellearning.com

ISBN 978-1-64040-077-1
Simplified Chinese Edition

About Level Learning:
Level Learning provides a literacy focused curriculum specifically designed for K-12 Chinese as a Second Language classrooms. Our program offers 20 levels of specific and detailed objectives, leveled texts and passages, mastery-based online assessment, and analytics to enable data-driven instruction. Level Learning reading curriculum for both literature and informational text emphasize grammar and comprehension skills to help teachers develop confident and independent Chinese language readers. The non-fiction series of books are specifically designed to support our informational text course based on multiple national standards. To learn more about our entire offering, visit www.levellearning.com.

About Washington Yu Ying PCS™:
Washington Yu Ying PCS is a Mandarin English dual language immersion International Baccalaureate (IB) World school. Yu Ying's mission is to inspire and prepare young people to create a better world by challenging them to reach their full potential in a nurturing Chinese/English educational environment. Yu Ying's comprehensive IB, dual immersion curriculum equips students with global competencies for success in the real world. As a leader in immersion education, Yu Ying is determined to advance Chinese language programs and global citizenry education by helping other schools create and strengthen their Chinese programs. For more information, email: products@washingtonyuying.org

有时候我觉得很难过，
有时候我觉得很开心。

有时候我觉得很生气。有时候我觉得很害怕。为什么会有这么多不同的感觉呢?

有时候我想大声叫。有时候我想大声哭。

有时候我想大声笑。有时候我想大声唱。

有时候我想用力跺脚。
这种感觉好奇怪。

老师说这些感觉每个人都会有。我们要学会知道自己的感觉。

生气的时候,我可以出去打打球、跑跑步。

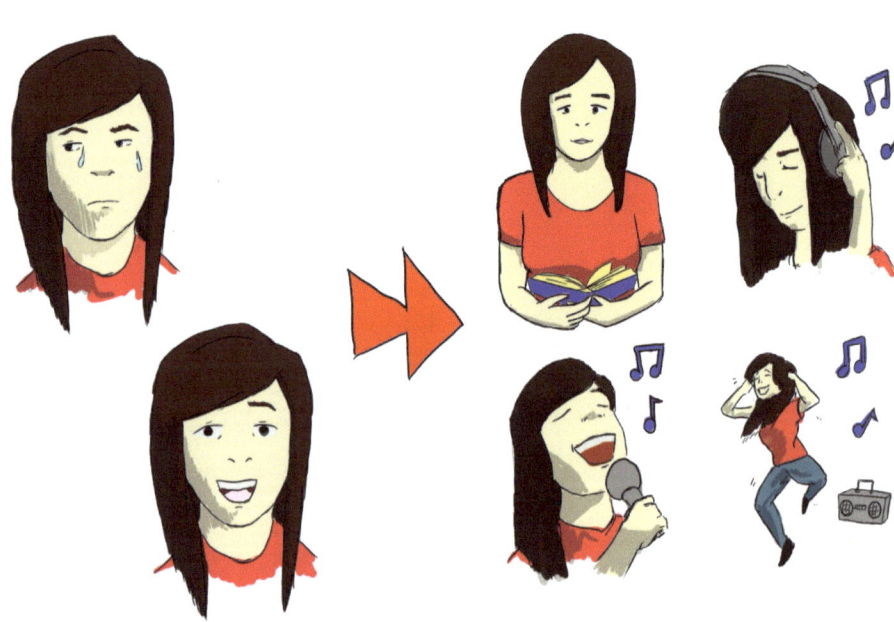

难过的时候,我可以看看书、听听歌。开心的时候,我可以唱唱歌、跳跳舞。

我可以抱抱喜欢的东西,也可以做做手工。我可以大声哭,也可以大声笑。

我可以告诉家人和朋友自己的感觉。

学会知道自己的感觉很重要。

Glossary

	Pinyin	English Definition
有时候	yǒu shí hou	sometimes
觉得	jué de	to feel
难过	nán guò	sad
开心	kāi xīn	happy
生气	shēng qì	angry
害怕	hài pà	afraid
感觉	gǎn jué	feeling
大声	dà shēng	loudly
跺脚	duò jiǎo	to stomp your feet
奇怪	qí guài	strange, weird
打球	dǎ qiú	to play ball
跑	pǎo	to run
听歌	tīng gē	to listen to music
唱歌	chàng gē	to sing
跳舞	tiào wǔ	to dance

	Pinyin	English Definition
抱	bào	to hug
做手工	zuò shǒu gōng	to work on craft
告诉	gào su	to tell
学会	xué huì	to learn
重要	zhòng yào	important

www.ingramcontent.com/pod-product-compliance
Lightning Source LLC
Chambersburg PA
CBHW041221070526
44584CB00001B/42